20-20

20-20

The top 20 tips
on the top 20 management
subjects

Contents

1

Time Management

1. Your life is only time- your time is your life. It's precious- you only get it once.

2. In order to manage your time successfully you'll need to be assertive and self-disciplined. All time problems come either from other people or yourself. Both assertiveness and self discipline can be greatly increased by having clear goals in your life.

3. Make a list of your personal and work goals. What do you like doing, that you would like to do more of? What do you want to achieve? Aim high. Make your goals clear and detailed so that you can see them in your head. Now you know what's important- anything that contributes to your goals.

4. Material things will not make you happy. To do and to be are more important than to have.

5. Aim to enjoy the present and achieve in the future. The past is gone and cannot be changed. Learn from it, but don't live in it.

6. Good time management will require you to overcome your Be Perfect, Hurry Up, or Please Others drivers- if you have any of these.

7. Make a master list of everything you've got to do. This will come from your goals (the tasks required in order to get there) as well as being things you've just got to do. Don't worry yet about when you'll do them, just put everything on the list. This is your raw material for planning- the first step towards taking control of your time, and therefore your life.

8. Allocate time every day to important but non-urgent tasks: planning ahead and doing things before they become urgent. All your results will come from this.

9. Saying no is vital- if you don't, your life will gradually fill up with things you don't want to do. Every time you let something new into your life something else must get squeezed out- and it might be something important. Don't feel guilty about saying no. Every time you decide to do something you effectively decide to NOT do everything else in the world. Are you sure that the thing you have decided to do is the best use of your time?

10. An alternative to saying no can be to negotiate- you can offer to do it later, spend less time on it, only do part of it, get help with it, etc.

11. Be assertive about interruptions and bad meetings. It's YOUR life that's being wasted. Assertiveness = courage + honesty. Have a no-crap policy in your life.

12. Empty your email inbox every day if possible, certainly every week – this will reduce your stress, give you a double check that all of the actions have been done, and also make it easier for you to find emails since they will all have been filed by customer.

13. Find a way to beat procrastination that works for you. Procrastination only affects important non-urgent tasks, which are the most vital ones! Procrastination is also a big contributor to stress. Good time management will give you a feeling of control and progress and will greatly reduce your level of stress.

14. If faced with a crisis ask why it has been able to happen and fix the underlying cause. Every crisis has an underlying cause. Most crises have happened before- don't let them happen again.

15. Have a jobs to do list every day. Not more than ten things, ideally only about five. This will focus you and you'll get much more done. If there are no urgent tasks to put on it then you can put on some getting-ahead tasks: even better.

16. Write everything down- either on your master list (I'll do it some time), your daily list (I'll do it today) or your diary (I'll do it on Thursday). If you promise something to someone, write the first step in your diary.

17. Diaries can be paper-based or personal organiser- whatever works for you. But they should cover both home and work in one, and be small enough to always have with you.

18. Never fill the days or weeks completely- allow space for urgent things that will crop up.

19. If someone promises they'll do something for you, ask when and write the date in your diary, and then you can follow them up when the date is due. They will soon learn to keep their promises when dealing with you!

20. Similarly, keep an email folder for "Did they reply?" so that every now and then you can check whether your emails got an answer.

2

Project Management

1. Define cost quality and time, in writing. If you don't get it in writing, at least an email, then there will be trouble a year later when other people have different perceptions of that they were supposed to be doing.

2. If you're not really sure what you're setting out to do then you'll probably suffer from people moving the goalposts during your project and possibly complaining afterwards that you didn't do what they wanted.

3. If you're being asked to do the impossible, for the good of your customer and yourself be assertive- remember that planning makes you stronger!

4. If there are a number of stakeholders who want different things then it 's a good idea to have a kick off meeting where you offer them a plan, or maybe a choice of plans – if they can't agree then that's their problem not yours. Don't start the project until everyone has said in public that they are happy with your plan.

5. Find out what's the key driver- is it cost quality or time? This is what you'll be judged on- the one area where you must not fail. Do this by asking your customer (or the various stakeholders) what they want, why they want it, and what will happen if they don't get it?

6. List the tasks. Be careful not to miss any! Do a group mind map, ask any experts you can find, look at history if previous similar projects have been done and draw up a structured breakdown diagram of all the tasks.

7. Draw the network diagram- this is best done by sticking post-it notes on a whiteboard, and this is the stage where you have to decide which tasks depend on which. In what order will you do the project? Put estimates of times on each task. This diagram will then tell you how long the

project will take- the longest route through the diagram is the critical path which is the quickest you can do the job.

8. Put in some contingency to allow for unexpected tasks and problems, in order that you still deliver on time. This will make your customer happy in the long run.

9. If the critical path is too long you might need to crash it- pick on the biggest critical tasks and think about reducing them by spending more money on them, or reducing their quality. There is always a price for doing something quicker!

10. Use the critical path to draw the Gantt chart. Start by drawing the critical tasks to scale, going diagonally down your chart. Put in the floating tasks wherever they fit between the critical ones.

11. Software: Microsoft Project is great for producing impressive Gantt charts, but it's expensive, has to be learned and remembered, and doesn't do resource planning very well, so I recommend good old Excel for your Gantt chart.

12. Think about resources / loading- by looking vertically down your Gantt chart you can see how many people you'll need at each stage- do you have enough people? You can slide floating tasks sideways to get rid of any horrible peaks, and you may have to extend the whole project (breaking the critical path) if you don't have enough people.

13. It might be a good idea to have a Gantt of Gantts for your area if not for the whole organisation, so that you can make sure that you can do all the projects that you want to. This would probably be on a spreadsheet with projects down the side and dates across the top, and resources in the sheet itself (e.g. hours of your time, or days of IT time required).

14. Consider risk- what are all the things that might go wrong?

Are they likely, or serious, or both?? How can you make them less likely to happen, or make the effects less serious if they do happen?

15. At the end of the planning process you might need to go back to the stakeholders and say "My plan shows that it's not possible to have what you want. Either you have to pay more, or wait longer, or live with a reduced specification. Which one do you want to choose?"

16. Once your project has started, monitor progress to your Gantt chart by colouring in the tasks as you complete them and seeing if you are keeping up with the "Now line". If you're starting to run late you can choose between leaving it as it is (= letting the plan slip) or crashing some of the tasks (money up or quality down) in order to catch up the time. Either way you need to issue a new updated Gantt chart, and check that the new timings are OK with those who need to do the work, and probably also the customer (even if you're still going to achieve the end date the costs and quality will probably be affected so the customer needs to know).

17. Compare costs with Gantt: if you are over budget but ahead of schedule that might be OK. More likely is that you are behind, so an underspend might not be a real underspend, just a sign of lateness. Even being bang on plan financially can signal a problem: you might be going at half the planned speed but spending at twice the planned rate! But these problems will be obvious if you've got a coloured in Gantt chart to show your progress.

18. Review- have a short meeting with your team, and ask "What was good / what was bad / what could we have done better?" This ensures that people get thanked, the organisation learns from its mistakes, and good practices get repeated (and even improved upon).

19. Consider having a post project review, maybe 2 years later. A project that came in on time and on budget may not have delivered the results that were hoped for (not the Project Manager's fault!) while a project that was over budget and late may well have given lots of benefits. The objective of this meeting is to get better at deciding which projects you do, as opposed to being better at doing them.

20. In any company it's a good idea to have a minimal paperwork system; forms for a) permission to begin a project, b) a plan c) monthly progress meeting d) control of all projects overview of spend and progress e) review. Without these you may get overlaps and conflicts between projects, visibility isn't clear across projects, and lesions won't be learned from each others' projects.

3

Leadership

1. The job of a leader is just to do three things – People Systems and Vision. To make sure you have the right people in the right jobs and motivated; to make sure that the systems are set up optimally and that they are working; and to generate and communicate a vision. That's it! But it's a full time job, and you must resist slipping back into doing your previous job because it's easier.

2. It is the number one objective of a leader to communicate a vision. The team have to know where they are heading, and to buy into that destination. You may want to consult and research before announcing it, but from then on it's yours. The plans about how to get there can be adapted over time, but the vision cannot.

3. Communication: tell people as much as possible about what is going on and why, both good and bad news. The more you trust them the more trustworthy they will become. Don't try to keep secrets- word will get out anyway and then you'll have lost the chance to be seen as the leader.

4. Anyone can be a good leader – it's about what you do rather than who you are. Admittedly the greatest leaders of history had charisma, but anyone can be a perfectly good leader. A key part of leadership is motivation- see separate list. Again, there are things do be done, which anyone can do.

5. Leadership is not quite the same as management – management is more about carrying out plans while leaders are more about generating the original vision. Management is more about the task while leadership is more about the people. But it's not worth worrying too much about the difference, since all leadership involves management too, and all management involves leadership too.

6. Build a team of different types: a good team needs a

mixture, including pushy people, detail people, creative people, pessimistic people, caring people, etc. You may not like some of these types, but you need them all.

7. Fairness is incredibly important, and the team will be looking out for any signs of favouritism. And of course there will be some people who you prefer or find it easier to work with. But you must fight the temptation to have favourites. The challenge is to share the work equally, apply the rules equally, and yet also to manage each person in the way that is best for them.

8. Have a weekly meeting with your team, so that you can maintain a grip of what's going on, so that they don't overlap what they're doing, and so that they feel like a team and they feel that you are their leader. Just half an hour will be enough.

9. Good leaders delegate rather than trying to do everything, or to make every decision, themselves. Micro management is very annoying for the troops because it sends the signal that you don't trust them. With a good leader the people say "We did it ourselves".

10. For every decision ask yourself "Who could I consult before making this decision?" or, at the very least, "Could I explain my decisions more to my team?".

11. Make decisions rather than avoiding them, and, when occasional mistakes happen, admit them.

12. Vary your leadership style according to the level of competence and motivation of each person. New starters need to be shown what to do, experienced under-performers need to be involved and consulted in order to increase their motivation, and those without either motivation or competence need to be coached: this means

encouraging and working with them to increase their skills.

13. Where is each person on the freedom ladder? Do they need to check with you before acting, or can they go ahead and do it and just let you know afterwards – or do they not even need to tell you each time but just give you a summary every now and then, for example at the end of each month? People need to k now clearly, for each part of their job.

14. For top performers: consider empowerment, which means not checking on them at all. Trusting them! Still be available for support, but only if they ask for it.

15. Ask for feedback and listen to it. Constantly strive to be a better boss. Don't let the power go to your head. Remember that 'Perception is All' so you can never say that what they think of you is wrong. If they think you could be better, you could be better.

16. Management by wandering about: spend half an hour a day seeing what's going on. This will allow you to put your message across, and more importantly to hear theirs. But don't get dragged into sorting out details- discuss any concerns (constructively!) with your line management on your return to your office.

17. Go back to the floor occasionally and remind yourself what the work involves. A day spent doing this will have all sorts of benefits- it sends a good signal, it allows you to take the temperature, and allows you to assess the details of the current methods and therefore to assess the quality of the management of those methods.

18. Forget about being liked. You can't please all the people all the time. Concentrate on being fair. You may have to make unpopular decisions, for good reasons. Getting rid of someone could well be one of these. Failure to take the

tough decisions will be seen as weak, and unfair (for example if someone is getting away with breaking them rules that the others have to follow).

19. Annually address the troops – talk to all of them in one go (if logistically possible) to talk about what's happened this year and what the plan is for next year.

20. Effective leaders will lead by example in all areas – honesty, quality, work rate, conforming to systems, customer focus. You have to be 100% perfect because everyone is watching you all the time, and the bad things get copied much faster than the good things. It is incredibly easy to teach a parrot to swear!

4

Marketing and Strategy

1. Marketing is not the same as PR. PR is only a small part of Marketing. Marketing is about planning your strategy: what will you sell to whom, and how will you achieve this?

2. Decide on your core skill, your "unique selling proposition", which will form the centre of your strategy.

3. Ask your customers what's important to them (these are your key success factors) and find out how you are performing on these.

4. Assess the structure of your current market: who are the customers, who are the competitors, and what are the current trends? Trends could be analysed in terms of political, economic, social and technological factors.

5. Michael Porter has suggested that are three main strategies that any company can choose from – Cost Leadership (being cheapest, or good value for money, e.g. Ford), Differentiation (being better, having higher quality, e.g. BMW) and Segmentation (aiming at particular niches where you can be a relatively big player and get established, e.g. Ferrari)

6. Segmentation is a way to understand your market – if you can divide it into parts that have different needs then you can make sure you are satisfying as many of them as possible. Segmentation can be by age, location, lifestyle, thought processes (imagine how newspapers target parts of the market), spend (e.g. supermarkets target people by spend) etc

7. Assess yourself within your market: what are your strengths and weaknesses, and what are the opportunities and threats out there? How do your strengths and weaknesses compare with the changes expected in your commercial environment? Do your strategies fit with the expected or possible changes in this environment?

8. Market share can be a useful tool for assessing your current strength and future growth potential. Absolute market share is the percentage of the whole market that you have – but markets can be hard to define and to measure, for example, are vans part of the car market? Relative market share is your size compared to the size of the largest player, and gives a useful distinction between concentrated and fragmented markets.

9. Assess your portfolio of products: which ones are in growing or declining markets, which ones are strong and weak in terms of market share and technological advancement? Where are the products (or services) in their product life cycle? Make sure you have some products that are early in their life cycle, or which have an advantage in a growing market.

10. Draw up a matrix of customers and products: do you sell all your products to all your customers (or types of customer)? Are some combinations of product and customer more profitable, and some combinations not worth the hassle? Maybe focusing would be worth considering? Who are your most profitable customers? And who are the customers, or types of customer, that have the most potential for growth, who are most secure, and the easiest to deal with?

11. Barriers to entry, which might be financial/investment or to do with knowledge, will affect your margins for your current products, the urgency to move on and design new products or services, and of course your ability to enter (and therefore the desirability of) new markets.

12. Think about your strategies for introducing new products (or services). Have you fully exploited your existing market, and sold every product to every potential customer in this market? Then, what new markets could you find for your

products? What new products could you develop for your existing markets? Be very careful about planning to launch new products in new markets- lack of knowledge can be a killer!

13. Diversification can be vertical or horizontal.   Vertical, upwards or downwards, is where companies go into the making of the parts they currently buy, or go into distribution and selling as well as manufacturing. Horizontal is where they start making or selling related products, e.g. a pen company selling ink as well.

14. Price: how much effect do price increases have on sales volume? Would it be worth putting your prices up? There are many pricing strategies, like charging less for the basic product and then more for parts or service.

15. Routes to market: should you be using distributors or agents, or setting up your own shops, or working on strategic partnerships?

16. Strategic Partnerships – these can be a fast way to increase your ability to reach new markets or perhaps also to get your costs down.

17. Economies of scale – in theory being bigger is also to be cheaper, whether it be buying or manufacturing or (though less so) providing a service. But there is usually an optimum point where the flexibility, sharing of fixed costs, and buying power of size are outweighed by the management effort, communication problems, complication and lack of individual ownership that you tend to get with a large organisation. So the question is "What is the ideal size for you to aim for?"

18. Promotion: how much should you spend and what's the best mix of advertising, exhibitions, direct mailings, sales force,

printed literature, partnerships, and the web?

19. How is your brand perceived? Is it worth investing in? Generally brands are more important for Business to Consumer than they are for B2B, but of course they are always helpful, the question is how much to spend.

20. Finally you'll need operational plans to put all this into practice- who will do what and when?

5

Change

1. Management IS change. If nothing changed then there would be no need for management, it could all just roll along the same every day. It's the job of managers to come up with ideas for improvements and then to make them happen = change.

2. People resist change because of fear of loss. It might be loss of knowledge power, loss of friends and social structure, loss of positional power, or loss of security. So the first thing is to reduce people's fears by involvement and communication.

3. Adapt to the type of people you are dealing with – some will want to know all the details, some will want a short summary of the benefits, some will want an exciting vision of the future and to talk to others who have been through it and who are now happy with it, and some will need to feel safe and will want you to spend plenty of time with them.

4. Planning the change – how fast do you need to do it? And therefore, how much involvement do you have time for? The more the better, but you may not have the time.

5. Who will you involve? Who are the key stakeholders, who has the power, who is going to be for or against? Can you use the ones who are in favour to help persuade the ones who are against?

6. A stakeholder map of power vs attitude (to what extent are they in favour) can be a helpful tool.

7. As much communication as possible, as often as you can, by a mixture of methods – meetings, emails, one to one, formal talks, intranet videos and blog, walking around, cascade down, etc. if you don't communicate then the grapevine will, and it's bound to be pessimistic.

8. Consider the influencing techniques (see other list) like

perceptual contrast (it's not as bad as...), scarcity (we need to hurry or we'll miss out), choice of evils, social proof (everyone else is doing it) etc

9. Plan the implementation as well as finding a solution – use project management techniques like Gantt charts for this. And of course, maximum involvement.

10. People go through a dip of denial and loss before coming out of the other side (hopefully) stronger than ever, and ideally they are helped through the dip by a) knowing it's coming and b) seeing a vision of how good it will be on the other side.

11. Force field analysis says that to make a change happen you need to a) increase the forces for change and b) decrease the resistance. These can be done by, for example, a) showing the existing problem clearly, maybe even increasing the pain of the existing situation, and then b) having a small pilot study done and showing that the new situation will be great.

12. Slightly different to force field is the idea of push and pull – rather than pushing (increasing the force on people to change) it's better to use pull techniques which reduce their resistance by understanding them and changing how they think about the situation.

13. Early successes can help a lot – publicise and build on the successful pilot tests.

14. Thin end first – start small and once you've started it's hard to go back.

15. Present a case based on money (you may have to be creative in how you convert things like wasted time and unhappy customers to pounds) and it'll be hard to management to

ignore. Even if the numbers aren't quite accurate, the point will be made..

16. Lewin's theory says that you first have to unfreeze the situation (get people to accept the fact that things have to change, then you make the change, and then you have to refreeze the situation – get the change embedded permanently and accepted by all as normal. This would include publicising the newfound benefits, including the new change as part of induction training for new people, and keep the new situation going after the change-makers move on by appointing new people to run it.

17. As organisations grow they go through four crises of change – the first is when the boss has to become a manager, the second is when the boss has to let go (it's too big for one person to know everything), the third is when there are too many mangers doing their own thing and the organisation needs to be controlled, and the fourth is when the organisation has become too bureaucratic and needs some empowerment brought in.

18. It might help to give the change a good name, one that has an encouraging ring to it without sounding like propaganda.

19. When planning a change it is worth doing a risk analysis – what might go wrong, how likely is it, and how serious would it be if it did? And then what are your plans to make these things less likely and/or less serious.

20. If you're on the receiving end of change, try to stay positive by thinking about what you can gain from it (learning if nothing else!) and by gathering as much information as you can about the new destination, having a number of options, and building a survival network of like-minded people.

6

Motivation

1. Give each person ownership of something- however small.

2. As well as ownership of at least one thing, give them involvement in as much as possible. This means involvement in your decisions!

3. Give people challenges to stretch them, as well as the work that they are good at and can do easily. Does everyone who works for you have at least one challenging project that they are working on?

4. Get people to set their own objectives- they will tend to be more ambitious than you expect, and will be more determined to achieve their own goal than one they got from you.

5. An annual or six monthly appraisal is very important to someone's motivation, because it clears up any gaps which lead to problems, for example "I think I'm doing OK but what does my boss think?" or "I think I'm weak at some things but is this a big or just a small problem to my boss?" or "I'm not sure what I'm supposed to be doing" or "I'm OK at the moment but where is it going?" or "I'd like to do more of X and less of Y".

6. Make sure that people feel secure. This comes from spending time with them, listening to them, explaining what the plans are, being honest with them, being supportive if they fail, and showing that you value them by thanking them.

7. Praise and encourage people whenever possible. Your objective is to build them up, and criticism just reduces people's performance.

8. Thank every person who works for you, every week. Find something that they have done that's good. If they don't do

anything exciting, you must still find something.

9. Coach rather than criticise: if there IS a performance gap then you do have to address it, but constructively. Start by asking if they know what to do differently next time, then help them with this if necessary, and finish by saying (and believing!) that you know they can do it.

10. Different people are motivated by different things to varying amounts. Find out what makes each person tick, & give it to them.

11. Give everyone opportunities for learning & then opportunities to use their new skills. I've never met a person who says they'd be happy doing a job that they were good at but weren't learning anything new (and I don't want to!).

12. Give people a feeling of progress & seeing results, which might be done by helping them plan small steps into a larger job, or explaining why something is being done so they have a vision of what they are working towards.

13. Involve people in their own development programme – what are their long term and short term goals, and what do they need to learn and do to get there?

14. Be a mentor and a coach, meeting occasionally with each person to check they are OK and that their development is going in the right direction. This is not quite the same as an appraisal, and certainly different to every day management.

15. Circles of potential – to what extent is the person fulfilling their potential? You can show this as four circles: what the job requires, what they are actually doing, their current comfort zone, and their untapped potential. Any differences in the four will mean something significant.

16. Some people need novelty, excitement in their jobs, and we

can't all have that all the time. But perhaps job rotation, and delegating more than you would normally, would give them more of this.

17. Some people need friendships & security, and a nurturing management style is important for them. Kicking them into shape is unlikely to be successful!

18. People like to feel part of a team, and this can be increased by making sure that the environment encourages it – a kitchen where people can cook or eat together, or a lounge area where people can socialise, is important.

19. Money is not a motivator! Insufficient money, or mistakes and broken promises, are certainly demotivators. But money does not make people care about their work. Money will make someone do something, but it won't make them WANT to do it. So: get the money right, but don't rely on it to motivate people.

20. Be aware of yourself as a role model. Are you always positive about the products, customers, and future? Are you positive when problems are reported to you? It's fine to admit to problems, but you must also be certain (and project certainty) that they are going to be solved.

7

Delegation

1. Delegation isn't just about giving out jobs to people when it's their job already – it's about giving out your job to other people. And it's easy to delegate things you don't care about – the real test is to delegate something important, that you really do care about.

2. Whatever your reason is for not delegating, it's false!

3. If they can do it 70% as well as you, or better, give it to them. Delegation is not risky if you keep an eye on progress and are there to offer support as needed.

4. Delegation means letting people do it their way without you interfering. This can be really hard to do if you are a perfectionist. Don't tell them how to do it, even if you know how – they must find their own way.

5. If you worry too much about whether they will have the time to do it, then ask yourself whether they could make just one more hour during the week to do something they really wanted to do (eat free doughnuts, see U2 playing in the pub across the road, etc) - and of course they could.

6. If you are so busy you don't have time to explain it to them, then you need to escape from the vicious circle and make the time!

7. Delegate to people who will find it a challenge and will learn from it and get a sense of achievement when they finish it, not just to someone who can do it easily. At least sometimes, start by thinking "What can I give Fred that will stretch him?", rather than "Who can I give this job to?"

8. You can always delegate part of a job if it's too big to delegate all of.

9. Anything routine should be delegated – it's a waste of you if it doesn't require creativity. Therefore you should routinise

(sorry!) as much as possible, so that you can delegate it. Bring in an expert system, a standard procedure with options and branches, that can then easily be passed to someone else.

10. Never let them walk away leaving you with the 'monkey' (This is when you say "Leave it with me")

11. Maintain a grip on progress by getting them to report to you regularly- the frequency will depend on a combination of how difficult and risky the work is and how competent they are at it.

12. There is no risk in delegating if you keep a close enough monitor on the job. Fear of it going wrong should never be a reason for not delegating something.

13. Management by wandering about: spending half an hour a day seeing what's going on will enable you to monitor the many tasks you have delegated, while also looking like someone who cares and is in touch with the people doing the real work.

14. You can only delegate to people who are both competent and motivated to do the particular job you are giving them.

15. For top performers: consider empowerment, which means not checking on them at all. Trusting them! Still be available for support, but only if they ask for it.

16. When giving out tasks remember that you can't please all the people all the time. Concentrate on being fair. You may have to give a job to someone who doesn't want to do it, in order to be fair. You MUST do this! Failure to make people do the jobs that you want to allocate to them will be seen as weak, and unfair (for example if someone is getting away with not doing one of the unpopular tasks).

17. When delegating, explain the importance of the task, and why the person is the best person to do it – either because they are great at it, or because they will learn something useful form doing it.

18. Make sure they know what the monitoring frequency and method will be. Maybe you'll meet once a week, or monthly, or maybe they are supposed to come to you when each part is completed, or only if there is a problem. But however you do it, they need to clearly understand it at the start.

19. When delegating, make sure the person understands what you want and is able to do it – this is easy to check, by asking them about how they will start on the task. Explain that support is always available, at any time, whatever the problem (or mistake) that has happened. If they don't feel supported they won't come to you and things can go horribly wrong.

20. Remember the benefits of delegation for you, and also for them – they get to learn, achieve, feel important, etc and you get time, a back-up, and the ability to be promoted without the job grinding to a halt.

8

Information

1. The life blood of an organisation is information, and managers spend most of their time gathering, assessing and dissemination information. Email, meetings, phone calls etc, are all exchanges of information. Most organisations have too much bad information (data is not information, and often it's unstructured, unsorted, and inaccurate) and there isn't enough good information.

2. Measure everything you want to manage – if you can't measure it you can't manage it.

3. When measuring one thing, ask yourself what else might be happening. Sales are up, but what's happening to prices and profits?

4. Always calculate ratios – they are much more useful that absolute values because you can then compare them. For example, rather than "total number of complaints" it's much more useful to measure complaints per person or per sale.

5. Compare ratios with similar areas, departments, and months.

6. Information should be used as a start for questioning not a conclusion for judging.

7. Swapping areas over will give you more information – for example if you change two managers over, or two sales people, or swap the ads between the two papers, you can work out whether it's the manager / sale person / ad or paper that's good or bad.

8. Don't be a slave to the numbers: a mixture of numbers and gut feel is best – beware if they don't agree!

9. Presenting a table is better than a load of text – it's much quicker to understand and clearer to interpret. Tables should be sorted on at least one of the columns, and include ratios.

10. Graphs are better than tables, usually.

11. When viewing graphs, beware of false bottoms – does the vertical scale go right down to zero?

12. Think about the graph or table from the users point of view – does it easily tell them what they want to know?

13. Beware of people's accidental or deliberate bias. Everyone sees the information from their own viewpoint, and we all tend to select data and a display method that suits us. When viewing information, as yourself "Are they being selective?"- selective time frames, selective comparisons, and selective one off examples can be used to make a point.

14. Are the numbers significant? Sales are up 5% but maybe they fluctuate randomly by up to 15% every month. Or maybe the only more 1% usually, so 5% is indeed significant. Significance means "it's very unlikely to happen by chance" – so a good way to test significance is to say "Could this easily have been just chance?"

15. "We are the number 1 investment company / toothpaste / customer-rated hotel". Remember that there always has to be a best, worst, top, bottom, increase, or decrease: but by how much?

16. Averages can be deceptive when distributions are not Normal, for example wages, life expectancies etc. Never add (or average) averages or percentages – always take the numbers back to the base real numbers and work out the average or percentage from there.

17. Humans are too quick to see trends – something must increase or decrease 8 times in a row before you can say for sure (95%) that it's a trend

18. Avoid forecasting the future based on graphs of history For example trends like S-shaped curves all look the same at the start, so you can't tell which one you are on until later

19. Trends depend on how far back you go – and it's very hard to know how far back to go. For example the UK has got hotter since the ice age, colder since Roman times when vines were grown, warmer since people skated on the Thames 200 years ago, so which one do you want to take?

20. Be very careful about assuming causation. If things are correlated it doesn't mean that one caused the other – maybe there is a third factor which is causing both of them? Maybe the second one is really causing the first?

9

Finance

1. Profit is sanity, Turnover is vanity.

2. The two main documents are the Profit & Loss Account (what happened in the last year of trading compared with the previous one) and the Balance Sheet (a snapshot of what the company owns, where it came from and where it is now). The P&L doesn't mean that much without the BS because we need to know how many assets were used in order to make that profit. A Cashflow Statement would be the third document to look at.

3. Profit is not the same as cash, and vice versa. If you haven't yet got paid, or you've been paid early, or you've just had a stage payment, or you've made lots of stock, or you are crediting yourself with half the profit on something that is half finished (at the year end) then you might be measuring the wrong thing. You need to track both.

4. Cash accounting is based on what you've actually paid to your suppliers and what you've actually received from your customers. Commitment accounting is what you've promised to pay your suppliers and what your customers have said they'll pay you. Both have their strengths and weaknesses.

5. Your debtors ratio will tell you whether you are good enough at getting your customers to pay you on time. Being bad at getting customers to pay promptly means that you have to have more working capital (=cost of borrowing it) and there is a greater risk that the customer will end up not paying at all.

6. Look out for cash flow problems if your company is growing – you will probably be tying money up in materials and stock as well as promotional activities and maybe extra people before you reap the benefits, and the cash to keep you going

can be significant.

7. Gross profit is what's left of your income after you've paid the direct costs (materials and direct labour). Net profit is what's left after the above plus your fixed costs – the building, the IT and other services, management, advertising etc. These tend to be 30-50% and 5-15% respectively.

8. It's worth thinking about elasticity of pricing – the effect of price changes on volume. For example, if you are making 5% profit and you put your prices up by 5% this will double your profit, providing you don't lose any sales. It would only be a bad idea if you were likely to lose 50% of your business from a 5% price increase – unlikely! Maybe it's worth putting them up by 10%, or more? Where is the optimum place? This is where you need to know the elasticity of demand.

9. Small changes can have big effects on profit. Raw materials and power, if bought more cheaply, can make a few percent saving overall, but if your profit is only a few percent then this can double your profit. Similarly, right control of wages can do this, but wages are different in that low wages mean unhappy people, quality problems, and high turnover of staff which is very expensive.

10. Return on Investment (RoI) and Return on Capital Employed (ROCE), while being slightly different, are both measures of how much profit you have made in relation to the amount of money you have put into the company. Basically, would you have been more sensible just putting the money into a deposit account and getting a completely safe return of 5% or whatever?

11. Net Present Value (NPV) is a way of allowing for the fact that profit in the future is not as valuable as profit right now, and payments in the future are not as costly as payments right

now – so you multiply/divide each year by a factor which gives you the value of all those future estimates and promises to you right now.

12. The gearing of a company is the ratio of debt to equity – so if you started by putting in only a small amount of your own money (or from shareholders) (= equity) and then borrowed lots then you are highly geared. There is a risk that if things go badly you might not be able to pay back all the debt from your equity reserves. Ideally you wouldn't borrow more than you have as equity, which is a gearing of 50%. Gearing too low is bad too, since you aren't driving the company as fast as you could be if you borrowed a bit more and invested it in marketing etc.

13. Companies for sale can be valued in two ways, which should approximately agree. One is a multiple of profit, maybe five years' profit (depends on the stability of the industry that you're in, but of course the problem is how many years to you take?) because this is what you'd actually get if you bought the company. Another is the actual value of the assets, i.e. buildings etc. But of course the problem with this one is that often the biggest asset is the customer base, known as Good Will, which is hard to estimate the value of.

14. When considering investing money in something, the usual way to decide is to look at the break even period – if a million pounds would then bring in £100,000 extra profit per year, then that's a ten year break even. A break even of more than two years is usually considered too long / too risky – even if it's certainly true and safe, there will be better uses for your money.

15. Prices are often based on costs, and costing is far from simple. For example, as well as direct costs like labour and materials you need to apportion some part of overheads

(fixed costs) to the product of service that you are costing – but how do you divide up the overheads? Does a department with more people need more management and IT and HR time? Not necessarily. Sometimes people use Marginal Costing, where you only take into account the direct costs. For example, selling a software CD for only £1 is still a profit since the disk only costs 20p. But of course this assumes that a) the development cost has already been covered by previous sales, or will be covered by future sales, and b) it won't drag all prices down to this level.

16. Depreciation is another aspect of the apportionment of costs – the idea being that if you buy a building or some machinery and it has a fixed known life, you spread the cost of the item over those years, and the value of the asset decreases over that time from the purchase price down to zero (or the sale price at the end).

17. Budgeting – the planning of income and costs in the future – the main thing is not to just divide the year by twelve. It's never that simple!

18. Valuation of stock – if a company has made a whole lot of stock, and the stock is certain to be sold, then it can be valued at the sale price and profit can be assumed to have been already made. But of course in real life you are never certain of selling it, you will be somewhere between likely and unlikely. So the question is what to value to stock at, and how much profit to claim. Sometimes companies have stock that has been given a value in their accounts, and each year it sits there keeping its 'value', but in fact it's worthless junk, but they can't throw it away because that would mean writing it off and admitting that the company has less value and the profits were lower than claimed. Having a high value of stock is good in terms of the company being valuable, but

bad in terms of money being tie dup unproductively – you don't get paid interest on your money when it's tied up in piles of stock, and in fact stock costs money to store and tends to decrease in value as it gets stolen, eaten by mice, and past its sell by date. A ratio that tells you about stock levels is Stock Turnover – cost of sales (i.e. turnover before markup) divided by value of stock held. High is good.

19. Liquidity is a measure of whether you can get your hands on cash if you need it. What if the bank wants its loans back? Your current assets are: cash that you hold, the money that is owed to you by customers, and your stock. These could be turned into cash if necessary. Your current liabilities are the debts you owe suppliers (in this ratio we don't count long term bank loans as debts, or fixed assets as assets, since they would take much longer to convert). If this ratio is greater than one you can pay off your debts if you needed to, so there is nothing to worry about. Sometimes stock isn't counted as an asset due to the doubts over its valuation, see above, and the time it takes to convert to cash.

20. Profit isn't kept by the owners and stuffed into their bulging pockets in wads of £20 notes. And it certainly isn't kept by the managers! So where does the profit go? The answer is that it gets re-invested as machinery and buildings and stock, and if not spent then it gets kept in the company's bank account and called Reserves. If you have shareholders then some gets paid out to them as dividends, which you may think they haven't worked for, but in fact they have risked putting their cash into the company at the start rather than putting it into a deposit account, so they at least deserve a reasonable return similar to a decent interest rate on their investment. If the company goes bust they lose everything, so if it does well they should get a share.

10

Cost Reduction

1. Reduce bureaucracy – how many forms are filled in and copied and filed that nobody ever looks at? Could they at least be shortened? Could fewer people be required to make a decision or check a decision?

2. Meetings – could they be shorter, fewer people attending, and more effective. Calculate the cost of a meeting, and then multiply that by the number of meetings in your organisation!

3. Measure and publicise the costs of everything – meetings, complaints, resources like operating theatres and trucks, raw materials and purchased items, etc Most people have no idea, or they just don't think about it.

4. Map your processes and then see if you can cut out or combine any of the steps.

5. Find the bottlenecks and attend to those. The cost of time lost at a bottle neck is equal to the cost of the whole system, while the cost of time lost at a non-bottleneck is zero.

6. Rather than only measuring costs, consider the cost benefit of spending a little now in order to save a lot over the coming years.

7. Pareto – 80 of your costs will be spend on 20% of your customers, 20% of your material line items, 20% of your problems, etc, so target the few expensive customers, items and problems.

8. Optimise your quality rather than just cutting it. Maybe improving your quality would save you costs overall in terms of reduced problems? Usually the point of minimum cost is not the point of maximum profit.

9. Measure, publicise and improve the utilisation of your assets. Are the Operating Theatres or the paint shop only 50% utilised?

10. Get an expert to look at your consumables – energy usage, waste removal and recycling, internet access, phones etc. If they are only paid on a proportion of provable savings, what have you got to lose?

11. Question the endless pressure for Reorganisations. These often cost more than they save. Better to measure the various areas, focus on the ones that are performing badly and sort them out. Leave the good ones alone!

12. Get rid of the right people. Not the most expensive, or the newest, or the ones who want voluntary redundancy, but the ones who aren't performing. Measure properly, prove it, and do it by the book.

13. Get a strong HR department so that you have complete and efficient support for the above.

14. Look at the cost of sickness and absence – it's huge! With the help of your strong HR, sort it out- either the offenders improve or they leave.

15. Look at the cost of staff turnover. It's huge! Can anything be done? Better motivation, better working conditions, fairer treatment, etc. you might have to investigate the reasons for people leaving first.

16. Get rid of some customers – there will be a bottom 20% who are actually costing you money, and another 30% with whom you are just breaking even...

17. Keep an eye on queues; if you reduce a resource by 20% the queues for that resource (which could be people or equipment) may well double, so it might not be worth making that cut. Queue length is equal to $U/(1-U)$ where U is the utilisation, so for 80% utilisation the queue length will be $0.8/0.2 = 4$.

18. A good IT function is vital, since bad IT is a huge hidden cost, holding everything else back.

19. Good purchasing and good negotiating can have a big effect on costs – some central purchasing departments don't really know what they are buying, or they buy what's convenient to them and not what the users actually want- and they tend to build themselves a cost nest of paperwork as security. But in principle it's worth taking purchasing seriously and if money can be made by centralising it and doing it really well, then so be it.

20. Engage your employees in the cost reduction process – they are the ones who know where all the waste is happening, and they are the ones who have to make the improvements.

11

Problem Solving and Decision Making

1. The best process is to start with a clearly defined problem, work out what the cause is (this might mean investigating a number of possible causes), and then come up with possible solutions and then select the best solution. The generating of possible solutions is a divergent thought process while the selection of the best one is a convergent process – these should be kept separate since they require different thinking, maybe even different people, and if you start judging suggestions then the suggestions dry up.

2. Consider how many people and who to involve, based on how much you know, how much you want to motivate the others, and how quickly you need an answer.

3. Getting the right cause – there can be assumed causes, multiple causes, and things that are correlated (happen together) but are not causes, e.g. being a rebel might cause both smoking and bad grades, but it is wrong to assume that the smoking is causing the bad grades.

4. A good way to identify the cause of a problem is to use the Kepner Tregoe process of "When does it happen compared to when it doesn't happen". E.g. Does it fail to print documents from only one computer? What happens if you swap the leads over?, etc

5. Finding a solution: Brainstorm as many options as you can. Remember to keep the judging till later. Even a hopeless idea can lead on to a better one from someone else, and the person who came up with it might come up with a better on if you encourage them to keep going. And remember that doing nothing is always one of the options.

6. Draw a mind map of the problem and the possible solutions – mind maps allow you get all the information out of your head so that your creativity isn't blocked, and they enable

everyone to share all of the information in a quick-to-understand format.

7. Draw a mind map of the problem and the possible solutions – mind maps allow you get all the information out of your head so that your creativity isn't blocked, and they enable everyone to share all of the information in a quick-to-understand format.

8. Draw a mind map of the problem and the possible solutions – mind maps allow you get all the information out of your head so that your creativity isn't blocked, and they enable everyone to share all of the information in a quick-to-understand format. Mind maps work really well because they use both the creative and the logical sides of your brain at once.

9. Edward De Bono's six thinking hats can be very useful when thinking about a problem. The idea is that you wear an imaginary hat, so for example the blue hat makes you analyse everything logically, while the black hat gets you think carefully about what might go wrong.

10. For decisions with many options you could use a decision tree, where each branch is an option, ideally with a probability of it happening and a value if it does happen (cost or benefit, whichever). You can then multiply the value by the probability (e.g. 10% chance of losing £1000 = £100) to decide which branch is most advantageous to choose. Often decision tree branches alternate like a chess game between the choices that you can make and then the things that might happen for each one, and then for each thing that might happen, the things you could do, etc.

11. When assessing options with multiple variables you can use a Rating Chart (the posh name is a multi-attribute utility

decomposition matrix) which you list the factors (reliability, cost of spares, performance in the wet, whatever) and then you give each factor a weighting – the more important the factor to you, the higher the weighting. You then give each option a score and then multiplied the scores by the weightings, and then add it all up. So for example the BMW might have a smaller boot than the Ford, but that has a low weighting, while it might have better performance in corners than the Ford, which has a high weighting, so when you add it all up the BMW wins. It loses on cost to the Ford, but how important is cost? – you must decide! Rating charts are good for helping you think, and for explaining your decisions, and for discussing group decisions, but they are still basically emotional rather than scientific.

12. Teams make better decisions than individuals – so although it takes longer, and not everyone can have what they want, it's always better to discuss decisions with a team, maybe using one of the above tools to give it a framework.

13. Look out for Risky Shift – teams make decisions which are more risky than those that individuals would have made. This is because within a team the more vocal people are usually the risk-takers, and also because accountability is shared so people feel more able to take risks.

14. Numbers vs. Gut Feel – which is best? The answer is that both should agree, and if they don't then you need to reappraise both: is your instinct wrong (can your planning win you over?) or is your local assessment incorrect – is there an error somewhere?

15. Occam's razor – if you can't decide between two options, then maybe that's because both options have the same value, and therefore it doesn't matter which one you choose. So take the simplest.

16. Sometimes none of the options are really good enough. In which case don't take the best of a bad bunch, but keep looking. Sometimes people list their decision-making criteria as must haves and nice to haves, in which case you must have all the must haves!

17. Try to relate everything to money. The cost of the current situation, the value of the benefits you will be getting after the solution is implemented, and how quickly does the cost of the solution pay back? Even rough costings are much better than nothing.

18. Risk assessment: when choosing between options, or even when you have chosen one, it's a good idea to look at what might go wrong, how likely is it to go wrong, and how bad would it be if it did go wrong? (Some people give scores to how likely and how serious and multiply these two numbers to get a "Should I Worry About It?" factor. And then of course you develop plans for making the problems less likely to happen and/or less serious if they do happen, and what really matters is the "Should I Worry About It?" factor AFTER you've taken these mitigation actions.

19. Sensitivity analysis is a form of risk analysis, where you look at how sensitive your solution (or your choice of solutions) are to the various risk factors. For example if a 1% change in the value of the dollar makes your deal a loss maker then that's much worse than a 10% change being needed.

20. Finally remember that a problem isn't solved until you've got an implementation plan of who will do what and when. Forgetting this has been the undoing of many a great idea.

12

Creativity

1. Keep going after the first solution, however good it may seem.

2. Reversal- Think about how to make it worse, then do the opposite. Think about doing the opposite to what you'd planned; are there any ideas to be gained?

3. 20 Ideas- Force yourself to write down twenty solutions, however ridiculous. Then, later, review them for the beginnings of ideas.

4. What-if- Follow some possible sequences of events, based on different starting points. What if the people were different, or if you changed the product, or the timing, or the method, or the promotion. What might happen? List the main features, then think about changing each one in turn.

5. Sleep on it- Just before you go to sleep, consciously and formally ask your sub-conscious for an answer to the question, to be given in its own time, when it is ready.

6. Matrix- Ensure that all combinations have been covered by drawing out a matrix combining the variables, for example, people with places, products with customers, markets with methods of promotion, etc.

7. Other people: one to one- Explain the problem to someone else. If doing this isn't enough to make you come up with new solutions, go through each of your ideas and describe the pros and cons of it. Describe what the ideal solution would be like.

8. Question the problem- do you really need to solve it? Do you really want to solve it? Is there a different problem you could solve, or a way to live with it?

9. What are the rules / the system / the convention? What if you didn't follow them?

10. What would other people do? How would they approach it? Make a list of people and their different approaches.

11. "Morphological analysis"- list the attributes of your starting point, usually as verb + noun (e.g. travelling on wheels, or powered by petrol). List alternative nouns for each verb. Make new phrases and combinations of these phrases.

12. Innovation transfer: transfer your situation to a different trade or market (e.g. butcher, doctor or teacher wants to cut costs, sell more, etc.). Brainstorm for them, then translate the ideas back into your own context.

13. Consult a fool- they could give you a new angle on the situation. The "fool" could be an untrained person, or perhaps a child / some children.

14. Think of some silly, fun solutions. Fun opens up the creative section of the brain. Do a brain-storm where only silly solutions are allowed.

15. What if the problem was a good thing? Where would that lead? e.g. what if it was good to be slow, or heavy?

16. Sacred cows: what are the fixed restrictions that will always be there? Now wheel these into the abattoir. How does that change things?

17. What is the second best solution? This forces you not to take the obvious or first choice. How can the second best solution be improved to make it the best?

18. Dictionary linking- Pick a word at random from a dictionary, and then think about how this word could be used in a possible solution to the problem. Or use adjectives from another noun, e.g. using cat on ships: cuddly ships, dead mouse ships, ships that stay out at night, ship flaps...

19. Chunking up or down: orange juice goes up to drink, down to beer, up to alcohol, down to Vodka, up to Made in Russia, down to fur coats...

20. Aim much higher than normal, e.g. to sell 100 times as much, or charge 10x as much, or employ 100,000 people. Now, how could you do this? Or if you had an army of 1000 people to help you, how would you do it?

13

Quality

1. Nobody knows that quality is! Some say it's in the eye of the beholder. While some say that it's an absolute. Some say it's doing what you said you would, while others say it's doing what the customer wants. Ideally you would cover all bases and make it something you agree with the customer and then always do.

2. Inspection won't give you quality. You can't inspect quality into something. Inspection (also known as checking or auditing) will find most of the problems that are worse than a given level, but it won't find all of them, and won't push you up above that level. It's also not very motivational.

3. Approaches to quality can be described as "Did we do it OK?" (Inspection – too late), "Are we doing it OK?" (Quality assurance, process control etc) and "Can we do it OK?" (Process capability). Clearly it's better to be ahead of the game, and taking a higher level view.

4. The UK has historically had a culture of "Good Enough" – if it's within tolerances then it's OK. The Japanese have a culture of "But why isn't it perfect?" which leads to continuous improvement.

5. An AQL is the Acceptable Quality Level- even if you want zero you may realistically have to live with 5 failures per million, and you may want to agree this level with the customer. Probably the tighter the guarantee the more it's going to cost.

6. Checking that you are within your AQL is difficult. 100% inspecting is expensive and still never 100% effective, so you're into the domain of sampling. If you sample too many you are paying too much, and if you sample too few you risk missing the few problems that are there. The maths of how many to sample is very horrible, since it depends on how

many faults there are, what the acceptable level of faults is, certain you want to be that you are OK or not, how accurate your estimate of fault levels needs to be, and finally, how homogeneous the population is that you are sampling.

7. Cost of quality divides into two parts – the prevention cost (stopping things going wrong) and the failure cost (putting right problems). Since PC goes up with improved quality and FC goes down with improved quality, the sum of the two is U-shaped. There will be a point of minimum cost at say a quality level of 5/10. however it is usually better to aim for 7/10 because for a small increase in cost (PC has gone up but FC has gone down) you can make your customers much happier and therefore either sell more or sell at a higher price.

8. A good start is to measure your failure costs. Many organisations don't even measure their failures (e.g. number of complaints) let alone convert these to money. Usually failure costs are invisible, while prevention costs (training, auditing) are clearly known, may even have budgets, so the pressure is always to reduce the prevention costs without realising that if you do this it puts up the failure costs, probably by more than you have saved.

9. Continuous improvement can be embedded in a culture by having regular continuous improvement team meetings where processes are examined and tweaked. Hundreds of small improvements can add up to a big difference in performance!

10. Quality Circles are groups of employees, ideally from all levels and areas, who meet to decide which quality problems to tackle and then to tackle them. They work on one project at a time, so they are not quite the same as a continuous improvement team who are looking at small changes to

everything.

11. Quality is about reducing variation. Variation is the root of all failures, as well as costing money. In order to get repeatability it is necessary to understand your processes, then measure the key inputs and outputs, and then control those.

12. Statistical Process Control is where you monitor a process by keeping a graph of both the mean and the variation, so that the process can be understood, and so that problems can be spotted before they get bad enough to affect the customer. This is much better than pass/fail, which doesn't distinguish between just passing and passing easily, and just failing and failing badly – and it can't see trends as the drift nearer to the failure line.

13. Management of quality depends on being able to measure the quality of what you are doing. This is easy when your widgets have to be exactly 12mm, but what if you are providing a service like a doctor doing an operation, or reception at a hotel, or if your product is bunches of flowers? Somehow you must reduce the product or service to measurable parameters so that you can then assess whether you achieving these. It is usually a good idea to consult the customer as well – what do they think are the important factors in a bunch of flowers? (Sometimes known as Critical Success Factors).

14. Research has shown that in the long term the higher quality producers tend to win. BMW will win over Ford, Waitrose will win over Tescos who will win over Aldi, etc. This is probably because those who go for the lower price option will sell more but they are operating under much tighter margins so they can't develop new products and services as easily.

15. One approach to managing quality is ISO9001 (which began life as BS5750) where the idea is to agree and write down all your procedures, and then make sure you stick to them. This is good for transparency and repeatability but some people feel that it reduces an organisation's ability to make continuous improvement small steps without lots of bureaucracy.

16. Another approach has been TQM – Total Quality Management – where the idea is to do everything right first time in all areas of the organisation, so that no time is wasted putting right other people's mistakes. It costs more to begin with but pays for itself later. The difficulty has been that it needs buy-in from the top, and often the top people don't want to get involved in quality management, especially if it requires money!

17. Ideally mistakes would only be made once, and to achieve this across the organisation would mean that all problems, and their solutions, should be recorded centrally so that everyone can see them. In order for this to happen you would need a No Blame culture – hard to achieve! Remember – no blaming, work on the system instead.

18. In order to avoid repeating mistakes it is necessary to get to the root cause – this involves asking why, probably more than once. The idea of the Five Whys is to ask why about five times will you get to the real root of the problem – which is often management!

19. For quality improvements to happen, people have to care. You can't force them to care about quality. Therefore it is necessary for people to have ownership of parts of the service or system, or at least be involved and consulted in the decisions that are made in their areas.

20. It is important not to let pressure for output / production / customers waiting / cost reduction cause you to reduce your quality standards.   This is usually achieved by putting someone in charge of just quality, completely separate from all pressures of operations, and reporting to the top person.

14

Customer Care

1. Customer Care is as important as the product or service itself. You are wasting your time getting the product or service right if you blow it at the last minute by rude staff, keeping someone waiting, not phoning the customer back, or whatever.

2. Organisations are judged in the first 30 seconds of contact with the first person who the customer sees. This may not be a highly paid or "important" person. But of course they ARE important, because of this.

3. The essence of Customer Care is making every customer feel important. Don't prejudge your customers by appearance. If they were the Queen, would you treat them like that? If not, there's a problem.

4. The first part of Customer Care is getting the basics right. These are the expected things – being on time, giving them what they have ordered, having clean and tidy premises, smart staff, etc. If you get these right the customers won't even notice, but if you get them wrong they will! You need systems and procedures for these, so they never fail.

5. Maybe the most important basic of all is getting their name right. To you it's just another word but to them it's the most important sound in the world. Double check it! Get them to spell it if necessary. If someone is called Stuart Thomson, alarm bells should ring! Twice!

6. The second part of Customer Care is the "delight". You need to think creatively about what you can do to delight your customers. These are the things they don't expect. These are the things they will tell their friends about.

7. After a while the "delight" things may become expected. Tough! You'll just have to keep on thinking of new delights for your customers!

8. Delight can mean remembering someone from last time – is their cat better now? Do they still take two sugars?

9. Delight can mean tailoring your service just for them – calling in to their house on your way home, making it a special colour for them, opening up your office on a Sunday morning especially for them, etc

10. Delight can mean little unexpected extras – the classic is the chocolate on the pillow, but it might mean "Do you want a (free) stamp with that?" or "We've included and extra copy in case you need it" or "It's closing time but we do have a take-away carton for your unfinished beer, if you want one"

11. Creative swiping – when you see something good, maybe you can copy it or adapt it to your own situation. Maybe a shop can copy a hotel, or a cruise ship, or a pub, anywhere is worth observing how they delight their customers.

12. Sometimes it's a Delight to bend the rules for a customer. This needs careful management, but is unavoidable. A Jobsworth can lose you a lot of customers.

13. Different people want to be treated in different ways. For some it's about being served quickly, for others it's about details, and for others it's about friendliness. Staff need to be trained to recognise these types of variation and adapt as necessary.

14. Customer Care is a management job. It is the job of management to recruit friendly people, set up systems, make sure the systems are followed, lead by example, and to get morale to a level where cheerful staff are motivated to care about customers.

15. Get people to care by involving them in setting things up, and giving them ownership of parts of the operation – at the

every least explaining to them what you're trying to do.

16. Only 4% of unhappy customers complain. This means that if you get 4 complaints you actually have 100 unhappy customers. And they have each told eleven others – so that's over 1000 people who have heard negative things about you. So those 4 complaints must be taken seriously. They may be difficult people but they bring an important message.

17. Customer Care is not just about new customers – it needs to be ongoing for existing customers too. The biggest cause of lost customers is "Perceived Indifference". Replacing a lost customer, i.e. getting a new one, is very expensive and difficult compared to keeping an existing one happy. Systems need to be set up to look after existing customers. And all staff need to be "Warm Fuzzy" types rather than "Cold Prickly".

18. Complaints can be turned into a net gain if they are handled well.

19. Customers need to be surveyed in order to find out what they think of you. This means existing customers, and if possible non-customers and ex-customers too. You need to know what they think is important, and how good you are at the important things.

20. Be your own mystery shopper occasionally. Try phoning in to your organisation. What are the first impressions like? Try queuing at reception. What does it feel like? How efficient are the systems?

15

Selling

1. The objective of selling is not to push something on to someone who doesn't really want it. It is to find out what they need and then to show them how you can help them.

2. People resist buying from people they don't like. So the game is to be as likeable as possible. We like people who a) make us feel important b) are similar to ourselves, so you need to a) compliment them and b) find out about them and show that you are similar, at least in some areas.

3. Make your compliments believable by adding either the reason or a question, e.g. " like that shirt, the double buttons on the collar are very trendy" or "I like that shirt, where did you get it?"

4. First impressions have to be right, so be smart and clean (shoes, fingernails etc), smile (so you look pleased to meet them), make good eye contact (so you look interested in them) and make sure your handshake is not too hard and not too soft.

5. Be a great listener. You can't help them unless you can first find out what their needs are. Other advantages of listening are that they will feel more important, they are more likely to like you, and also that you have control of the conversation if you are asking the questions.

6. Use the questioning funnel- start with open questions, then move on to probing questions like "How do you mean exactly?" and "Tell me more".

7. Put a little comment in between each answer they give and the next question you ask, just to show that you've listened, (indeed, to force you to really listen!) and to make it feel like a conversation rather than an interrogation.

8. Adapt to each of the four types: Analytical, Controller,

Enthusiast, Amiable. They want to know about details, saving time, novelty/fun, and safety respectively.

9. Link your solution to the customer's needs: once you know what they want, you can select the best solution for them, and show how the solution that you recommend will help with these needs.

10. Only talk about the features that will benefit them – the customer doesn't want to hear about everything when most of it is of no interest to them.

11. Prepare a features and benefits chart, so that for any benefit that the customer needs you can look up (in your head) the features that will give them that benefit – you can then say "We have features X and Y which means you'll get benefit Z"

12. Objections, if any: The first objection they come up with is often not the real one so there's no point trying to overcome that. Find out the real objection by peeling the onion- "Apart from that...." For example "apart from the price, is it perfect for what you want?"

13. There are many other ways to overcome objections. Make sure you know what the commonest objections are and have answers ready. For example, answers to the price objection might be cost per use, cost over time, benefits outweigh cost, other alternatives cost more, safety, essential to survival, intangibles which you can't put a cost on, etc

14. A useful way to overcome objections is by using feel/felt/ found: "Yes, I know how you feel, in fact I felt the same way at first, but what I found was..."

15. Consider a third party version of feel-felt-found: "Yes, good point, many customers worry about that to start with, but what they always find is... Would you like to talk to someone

who has had the same experience?"

16. Close: ask for the order. Ideally the close would not be sudden but a gradual crossing of a line where buying slowly becomes inevitable. Have a favourite close and use it comfortably.

17. After the sale make sure they are left feeling comfortable with their decision.

18. Keep in touch with them for referrals and future sales. These are much easier than getting new customers.

19. If you don't make the sale keep the next action with you, so that you have a reason to call them again.

20. Efficiency: always be on time, always bring the things you need, prepare information on the customer, have a system where you always keep your promises, phone them back when arranged, no spelling mistakes, etc.

16

Negotiating

1. If you don't ask you don't get. Remember that by negotiating you are never going to cause yourself to lose the deal, providing you are nice and you are prepared to crumble.

2. Instead of saying no, why not offer a trade and see if they are prepared to make it worth your while? If they can't, then it's them that are saying no, not you.

3. Avoid fear and embarrassment by thinking of the negotiation process as a game. Observe the other person, and learn from both good and bad opponents.

4. Aim for a win/win outcome where tradeables can allow you both to gain. Prepare the things that you can easily offer them which they will find valuable, as well as the things that you want from them that they could easily give you. The more tradeables you can prepare, the better- try to have at least thirty.

5. Set your walk away point and NEVER go beyond it, even by a small amount. This is the source of all your strength. If you have to walk away then you'll be stronger next time because you KNOW that you can walk away. Your walk away point is not determined by the market rate, it is determined by your personal situation.

6. Prepare their possible weaknesses to make yourself feel stronger. Put yourself in their situation. Think about their weaknesses rather than your own. Ask them questions to confirm the existence of these weaknesses. Don't be intimidated by sole suppliers – they still have weaknesses, like fear of competitors that you don't know about, individual sales targets to meet, etc

7. Always be nice, whatever the other person is doing. Nice, but steely and scientific underneath.

8. Ask questions and listen- the more you talk the more you give away. The more you find out the more you will gain.

9. Try to avoid opening first. Their opening offer might be good news, and whatever it is you will gain information and can modify your opening position accordingly.

10. Open wide. Your opening offer should be just beyond the best you could hope for, otherwise you'll never get the best.

11. The Flinch – look for a reaction when you put your opening offer on the table (no reaction means you didn't go far enough, so don't move from there) and also, make sure YOU give a reaction when THEY open. Negotiating isn't about hiding all reactions – if you don't react they will think their opening offer wasn't wide enough.

12. Don't open with a round number. A more precise number sounds scientific, as if it's already your limit, and from there you can more in small amounts.

13. Move in small steps. Large steps give more away, and imply that you've much more still to give, and also they make your opening position look dishonest.

14. Look out for, and use, The Vice, where you say "You'll have to do better than that I'm afraid". The Vice is usually a buyer's tactic. The answer to it is "How much better exactly?" (In other words, get them to open).

15. Never concede unilaterally, giving things away to make them happy with you. This just makes you look weak and makes them ask for even more. Instead, trade using the format "If you... then I..."

16. Look out for The Salami – where they ask for lots of small concessions that all add up (a slice at a time). Fight back by saying "If you want that then you'll have to give me X" or "If

you want that then you can't have the other slice that I agreed to just now".

17. Never use the phrase "final offer", either as a statement of as a question. If you ask them if it's their final offer they will have to say yes, and then they can't move – you have closed the door on any future progress. And if you use it then next time they will wait till you use it, so you have lost your ability to manoeuvre.

18. If they offer to split the difference it means that they have already given up, so the best answer is "No, I'm afraid this is as far as I can go".

19. Watch out for the Nibble, which is when they introduce something extra after you have reached agreement. Be prepared to call off and restart the whole deal if they try this.

20. Review- did it go to plan? What did you learn?

17

Influencing

1. Start with a clear objective

2. It's better to use pull methods rather than push. Pull methods are about changing what the other person thinks so as to reduce their resistance, while push methods are about increasing the force towards what you want. Pull methods are a bit harder to plan, but they carry on working after you have left the scene.

3. Be liked. Key factors in this are having friendly body language (especially smile), being a great listener (only talk about yourself for 10% of the time!), and complimenting others (genuinely!).

4. Make your compliments believable by following the compliment with either a question (I like that shirt, where did you get it?) or an explanation (I like that shirt, it's a really unusual blue) – or both.

5. It is essential to understand the other person. What's in it for them? Imagine being them - what would convince or motivate you if you were them? Use questioning to find out what will make them change their position.

6. A good questioning format is the questioning funnel. This starts with open questions (How do you feel about....) and then moves into probing questions (Why do you think that? And then what happened?) before finishing with closed questions (So do you want to do it then?). the probing questions are where you get most information. They are improvised, but have a fairly standard format. Practice them and get good at them.

7. Adapt to each of the four types: Analytical, Controller, Enthusiast, Amiable. Logic only works with some people. If they are a facts person, confront them with a detailed factual record.

8. But often feelings can be more powerful than facts, since they cannot be argued with. Consider saying honestly how you feel. Feelings can be especially powerful with someone who normally uses logic.

9. Reciprocity – if you do a favour for someone, however small, they are then much more likely to agree to what you want because they feel that they owe you. Debts must be repaid! Ideally you would do nice things for people all the time so that if you need to influence them later, you have more chance.

10. What you say may not be true. What they say must be true, to them. So use questioning to get them to say what you want. (e.g. "How would more exercise improve your life?").

11. Involve them in helping solve the problem. Ideally they will feel that the solution is theirs – or at least partly theirs.

12. Consider making the situation more painful for them (perhaps by doing nothing) so that they have to agree to making changes of some sort, preferably the ones you want.

13. If you can show that something is scarce, or might become scarce / run out, then it suddenly becomes much more desirable. "I only have two dates left in October" – you know you want one of them!

14. Sometimes offering them a choice of two evils works better than offering them one yes-or-no evil.

15. Suggest a small, easy, trial first step. Cautious people, or lazy people, will prefer this.

16. If you can compare your costs with something much larger (like the savings they will make, or the amount they spend on something else) then your figure looks small. Similarly if you can compare the savings with a much smaller number then

the savings will look larger.

17. Social Proof – if others think it's a good idea then it must be, especially if they are similar to the person you are influencing. For example "We are running this course for ten other local authorities" or "Look at Mile over there, he's exactly the same age as you and he's loving eating that delicious broccoli"

18. What objections do you expect them to come up with, and how will you handle these? Probably four objectives make up over 80% of the objections you'll get. Price is one that has to be on your list.

19. Discover the real objection by peeling the onion- "Apart from that..." They may not come out with their real objections straight away, and price is often one of these dummy objections which you can get past by saying "If we could sort that for you somehow, would you buy it?". Then we can get to the real thing that is worrying them.

20. Overcome objections by using "I know how you feel, I felt the same way (repeat some of their statements), but what I found was...". The third party version can also work well: "Yes, good point, in fact many of our customers think it looks expensive when they first get the cost, but what they always find is that after a year it's really worth it – look, I've got some references here"

18

Networking

1. Wear smart clothes – if in doubt go towards the smarter end of things

2. Get there early (and eat a mint just before you go in)

3. If you're there with a colleague, split up.

4. Avoid any free alcohol – this is work! And don't eat loads, it looks bad. Hold a drink so that you look involved, but don't drink it.

5. Stay standing, never sit down. Stand at 45 degrees so that people don't feel too threatened.

6. Don't prejudge people by appearances

7. The first 5 seconds are all about body language: smile, eye contact, and the right handshake – not too hard, not too soft, not clammy, not weird in any way. Perfect your handshake, and get someone to check it for you just to make sure.

8. What is your approach line? E.g. "It's an impressive turnout isn't it?" or "I think I know most of the people here but I've not meet you before have I?"

9. Introduce yourself clearly – many people mumble their own name.

10. What will you say when asked "And what do you do?". Plan your 'elevator pitch', including what you can do for them (I help people to...), and your hook/USP

11. Always have your business cards with you – how many can you give out? Keep your cards in a case – make sure they aren't dog-eared or even the slightest bit bent or creased.

12. Ask everyone for their card – see how many cards you can collect. Treat the cards that you receive with interest and

respect, don't just stuff them in your pocket without looking at them, but ask questions about them.

13. Be impressed by their card / job title / company / self-employedness – something!

14. Talk first, look at their name tag second

15. Be interested in them – don't worry about talking about yourself – prepare some generic open questions

16. Don't overstay your welcome with each person

17. End with a call to action (e.g. "Call me if you ever....")

18. Write notes as soon as you've left each person, or as soon as possible after. So you'll need a pen! Maybe write the notes about the person on the back of their card.

19. Send them a "Pleased to meet you letter/ e-mail" afterwards, ideally personalised with some reference to the conversation you had

20. Keep in touch – even (especially!) if you don't want anything from them at the moment

19

Presentation Skills

1. Start your planning by thinking "What's my one central message?" Your whole presentation should be designed around this, and should keep referring back to it.

2. Use a mind map to plan the structure of your talk – get everything down first, then think about which branches in which order, and how many sub branches for each topic.

3. Prepare your first minute really carefully- once you're off to a good start you'll be fine.

4. Talk to the audience as they arrive, so that you are relaxed before you start your talk, and so that you have an initial understanding of their mood and thought processes.

5. Look smart, professional, and boring! Resist anything wacky or sexy since you don't want the audience being distracted from your message.

6. Imagine the presentation going really well. Say to yourself that you enjoy doing talks because you're good at them and they always go really well.

7. Stand up to do your presentation, even if it's only to two people. Use a flipchart as an excuse to stand.

8. Bring a spare everything – pens, extension lead, notes on a memory stick or CD, etc – this will make you more reliable but also mean you have less to worry about, so you can concentrate of the most important thing, the talk itself.

9. Ensure equal eye contact for all, especially those at the ends and corners.

10. Show an agenda at the start, and frequently refer back to it so they always know where they are in the 'tunnel'. Then signpost your progress as you go through the agenda: "OK, that was section 2, 'Preparing', now let's go on to section 3, The Meeting Itself"

11. Your introduction should include an answer to the question that all of the audience will be asking themselves: "What's in it for me?"

12. Be interactive - ask the audience questions as you go along. This keeps them attentive, and also allows you to adapt the speed and content to their needs. It's also nice to know that they are still with you.

13. Use examples to make abstract ideas come to life.

14. Always use a visual aid: flip chart, OHP, PowerPoint, whiteboard, or just notes placed in front of them. Select the right visual aid depending on audience size and the level of formality of the talk.

15. Get a bluetooth remote controller so that you can walk around and advance the slides without having to press buttons on the lap top.

16. To remind you of your next point use bullet points written in large writing on a sheet of A4 and placed on a table in front of you. Don't use cards, and never read from a script. Using your visual aid to prompt you is the best way of all.

17. Keep the slide show as visual as possible, with lots of pictures and diagrams and minimal text.

18. Allow for the fact that people will have 'microsleeps' where they drift off for a few seconds, maybe thinking about what you've just said, or thinking about something else entirely. This means you'll need to repeat the main points, and if everything is visual then the microsleepers (whose eyes are still open!) can see the words on the screen, and it also makes it easier for them to rejoin the talk when their concentration comes back.

19. Plan how you'll finish- probably a summing up with a call to action. Rather than fizzling out, your talk should have a "stand up and applaud" finish.

20. Finish on time – this means planning your talk, probably only having one slide per 5 minutes, having a run-through, and perhaps having a section near the end that you can miss out if you need to.

20

Assertiveness

1. A person can change if they want to – most of our behaviour comes from our attitudes and beliefs which have been collected over the years, and which are stored in our subconscious. We can choose to change our behaviour, and we can also (gradually) change our beliefs about the world and about ourselves.

2. Assertiveness is difficult because it goes against our natural instincts for fight or flight. We have to learn to make a conscious effort to overcome the adrenaline in our bodies and remain calm.

3. A good step towards being assertive is to realise that the perceived benefits of being aggressive or submissive are in fact incorrect. Aggressive people think that they will be respected and will get their way – not true in the long run. Submissive people think that they will be liked and will have an easy life – also not true.

4. Assertiveness requires a starting belief that you are OK- which you are! Your self worth should come from you, not from what other people think. Think to yourself "No-one else can push me into the not-OK box".

5. Assertiveness means standing up for your rights, but also respecting the rights of others.

6. Persist if necessary. You have the right to be heard. You're not being rude, they are.

7. You have a right to say how you feel. And you don't have to justify how you feel.

8. Take responsibility for how you feel, what you do, and what happens to you. "We teach others how to treat us". Lack of taking responsibility is at the root of all negative emotions.

9. Take responsibility for mistakes. It's OK to make them (the

only way to never make a mistake is to never do anything, and making a mistake doesn't make you a bad person) but you must learn from them. Then let them go- they are in the past.

10. Your behaviour is controlled by your subconscious beliefs, or "scripts". You can change your scripts by what you say to yourself- keep it positive. Saying positive things about yourself repeatedly will gradually convince your subconscious that they are the case – anything you say regularly will become true.

11. You can change your behaviour, but only if you are aware of it. Practise detachment- observe yourself in situations: how did you do?

12. The other side of detachment is that other people are responsible for their own actions. Don't blame yourself for the actions that others have chosen to take.

13. Remain calm in situations where the other person is being aggressive. It's their problem not yours, so remember your rights, and take time to plan. Don't get aggressive back!

14. Aggression can be behaviour other than physically attacking someone- it can be verbal intimidation, interrupting, invading someone's space, patronising, etc. If someone is using emotive words to attack you, pick them up on the words: "I agree that it was a mistake but I wouldn't say it was 'stupid'."

15. Pick them up on aggressive body language using the format "I notice that you are doing xxx and I interpret this to mean yyy, am I right?" This will force them to put up or shut up.

16. When criticised, consider whether they may be right. If they are: learn from it and thank them. If they are not, you can

choose between letting it go or challenging them- both are OK. If you unsure about what they are unhappy with, or if you are unsure whether they are right about it, ask them for more information.

17. Giving criticism is not usually effective because asking someone to change their personality is not feasible, and it's even worse if you don't say what you want instead. However, asking someone to change their behaviour CAN be effective.

18. Look out for Games Players, who move between Persecutor, Rescuer and Victim (for example I'm Only Trying To Help You, Yes But, It's Alright For You, You shouldn't let him get away with that, etc) and then either refuse to play, be assertive about their behaviour ("I don't like it when you...") or expose the game ("Have you noticed how you....?").

19. Use the 4-step process to make your point: I understand, I feel, I want, Is that OK?

20. Wish you'd said something at the time? Don't worry- it's never too late to go back & be assertive. Plan it and then do it.

Well, that's your 20 subjects!

But I just can't resist adding a couple of other subjects which I think are pretty important – I hope you enjoy them too....

Success

1. Be yourself. This requires courage and honesty, but if you're not yourself you can only be diminished – you can subtract but you can't add.

2. Positive self- talk: tell yourself that you can do it rather than "It'll never work, I'm not good enough etc"

3. You reap what you sow, so help others to succeed with you.

4. Be interested in other people – they all have something to offer.

5. Be a great listener – ask people about themselves and their plans. Who knows where these conversations will lead?

6. Keep in touch with people – be a collector. They'll all have their time when you'll be glad you met and kept them.

7. Be ruthless with your time. If you don 't enjoy something and it's not getting you towards achieving your goals, don't do it.

8. Be efficient – have lists of what you plan to do, and use them.

9. Be reliable – this means keeping y our promises, being on time, and delivering promised work on time.

10. Be easy to get hold of and always call people back. Why fall at an easy fence like this one?

11. Have clear goals for home and work, so that you know where you're going.

12. Enjoy paying the price to achieve these goals – the price is part of the process.

13. Plan the steps towards achieving these goals, ideally with dates.

14. Enjoy the journey of life as well as the arrival – life IS the

journey. Part of your goals should be to have journeys that you enjoy.

15. Live in the present and plan for the future, and don't give the past too much attention. Yes you can learn from it, but you can't change it, and you can't go back to it. So don't' waste time on regrets and if onlys.

16. Volunteer for challenges and try new things. It's good for you to come out of your comfort zone. It makes you stronger and more skilled.

17. Choose who you associate with. Avoid negative people and choose people who build you up and stimulate your mind.

18. Set up a mastermind group who meet to discuss life plans, challenge and support each other.

19. Look after your health – exercise and sleep, and not too much booze.

20. Read lots of books – all the world's knowledge is in there, so why try to reinvent the wheel?

Happiness

1. What gave me pleasure recently that I could do more of?

2. How can I get more time for the good stuff? What would I like to get rid of from my life? Can I make the chores more fun?

3. What's my favourite negative emotion – and what is the pay off I think I get? Do I need to reduce the amount of guilt I feel, and if so, what is my plan?

4. Could I take responsibility more for what I feel and do, and for what happens to me?

5. When doing what could I say to myself "This is the life!" ?

6. Try meditation

7. Have a clear-out.   And then maybe try compacting – not buying anything (except essential food!) for a fixed period.

8. What childish activity can I do more of?

9. How can I get more of Nature into my life?

10. How can I increase the amount of sleep I get? (e.g. reduce TV)

11. How can I get more exercise? – what type, and when?

12. Friends – who is for the chop? (or at least reduction). Who will I spend MORE time with?

13. How can I give a bit back? Charity, helping friends, etc

14. Am I too obsessive about trying to master anything? What new activities could I take up, and dabble in?

15. Am I too competitive about anything that I do?

16. Am I learning anything at the moment? What could I start?

17. How can I increase the level of security that I feel?

18. What can I do to come out of my comfort zone? Can I diarise some challenges, some learning and some fun?

19. What can I add to my life that's creative?

20. Make a playlist of music that you like and which is cheerful

.

This book was produced by

Chris Croft

Chris runs training court

Time Management
Project Management
Customer Service
Leadership
Negotiation
and other subjects

he can be contacted on

01202-747480

34 Parkstone Heights

Poole BH14 0QF

www.chriscrofttraining.co.uk

chris@chriscrofttraining.co.uk

Chris Croft

www.ingramcontent.com/pod-product-compliance
Lightning Source LLC
Chambersburg PA
CBHW051202170526
45165CB00015B/2105